Yearnings Of A Troubled Dream

Krishnakamal M

BookLeaf Publishing

Presentation by *BookLeaf Publishing*

Web: www.bookleafpub.com

E-mail: info@bookleafpub.com

ISBN: 9789357215695

First edition 2023

DEDICATION

I dedicate this book to my parents, M. Madhusudhanan and Latha K. G., and to my friend Aleena Anabelly A., without whom I would have never written this book.

ACKNOWLEDGEMENT

I want to thank my friend Aleena Anabelly A. for informing me about this competition, as well as for encouraging me to write more and more poems, and for her honest and constructive criticisms of my work. I would also like to thank my parents, M. Madhusudhanan and Latha K. G., and my sister Krishnakavya Madhusudhanan, and also to Sarath Chandran, my brother-in-law, for all their love, care, and support, ever since the day I was born.

PREFACE

I have never really delved into the art of poem writing, nor do I consider myself a proper poet. I wanted to write about things that were on my mind at times when I was at my low points. These writings came out in a form that could be considered close to that of a regular poem, which is what you will witness in these twenty one poems.

The Stolen Words

Of poems written through my hand,
A hundred ideas made true in ink.

Are they all mine or someone else's?
Lost ideas I reclaimed as my own.

Original so they seem in my mind,
Yet could have been thought of before my time.

Am I a thief of time, picking ideas that never bore
fruit?
From minds lost to history, remembered no more.

Will the words of my pen ever be my own?
Or will they all be written by ghosts of the past?

Am I simply a tool to be used?
A chisel to shape a forgotten memory?

A fool of a slave tied in strings.
A puppet dancing to a hymn, so new and yet, so old.

My ambition serves me no regrets.
My arrogance grants me no deliverance.

A thief is all I am, timeless,
Wandering for thoughts from the forgotten dead.

The Tree

The tree stands still, in spite of the wind.
Colourless and lifeless, yet stands still.

Its leaves of dim grey,
and its bark one with earth.

My heart aches as I near the tree,
My eyes with tears and my brow with hate.

Its roots go deep into the Earth,
And the others tie me all around.

My rusted blade, so sharp,
I swing at them with haste.

With every cut I make in two,
My blade turns blunt and thoroughly used.

The Tree looks back with a familiar face,
Its crooked smile, so evil and cunning.

The Tree looks back with a younger face,
Of eyes with tears, filled with forgotten dreams.

A final root is clutched around me,
Weak and withered, yet with a pull so strong.

I try to fight, with a pull of mighty force.
The root fights back, with force a bit more.

Am I never to be void of this Tree?
My shadow casting over me forever.

I have lost to this Tree, never to be forgotten.
Why did I ever plant this forsaken Tree?

Greed

Is greed what drives us forward?
The very essence of all progress.

To want more that what we have,
To look further than our eyes would let us.

To seek what shouldn't be found,
To taste of which is forbidden.

To be satisfied is to be dead,
And we never stopped being alive.

We killed, tortured, maimed and fought,
Our legends etched in stone and songs.

We came unto Earth where all there was,
And we return to dust with nothing left.

A greed shortsighted, yet, of power,
Unstoppable and is the human spirit.

What's to life without greed?
To be content and happy of what is? Never!

The Artist

An artist of numb fingers and swollen eyes,
Sunk in their work of endless passion.

How does an artist know when to stop?
To end their craft, fully content.

Does an artist ever turn content?
To know that their work cannot be perfected further.

Or is an artist cursed to never be content?
To never feel satisfied in their magnum opus.

The last stroke of the brush, the last word etched in
ink,
The last curve in the marble, the last note to be
played.

A true artist is never content,
For their art is never perfect.

The pursuit of perfection, to seek its sublime form,
It's the journey of art for all artists to attain.

Dreaming the Girl at the far end of the Lake

O' Maiden who calls to me,
In my dreams of every night.

The air so cool, yet gentle.
The sky so blue, yet bright.

The lake so still, yet with rhythm.
The bright moon painting it with its bright smile.

Your eyes an artist's painting of the Lake.
Your hair so dark with a hint of blue.

Staying at the far end of the shore.
You flaunt your beauty to the envy of the moon.

Your figure a captivating form,
Covered in your dark apron.

To withdraw my eyes, I cannot,
The moon a crescent laying on your lips.

Oh, to be in your embrace,
No matter the horrors that await me in it.

You utter not a word, yet mean so much.
Your eyes so vague, yet so piercing and
dominant.

Your form radiating an icy warmth,
To which there may not be an end.

Your nails so sharp, yet smooth and shaped,
I feel your taunting at the sides of my neck.

Does your bosom chant your heartbeats or mine?
Or does it hold no heartbeats at all?

My Mistress, the Girl at the far end of the Lake!
Hold me in your everlasting embrace!

Murder

What does it take to murder a person?
To take their life and douse their flame.

A billion chances to be born.
A billion more to see it to its end.

And yet to have it taken so soon,
To not see to the end.

To take those moments they cherished and
enjoyed.
To tear them away those they loved and cared
for.

To pluck out the eyes before it could see.
To have them rot in their prime of ripe.

On the precipice to contentedness, their journey
cut short.
My icy cold hands, rips their dreams to shreds
aloft.

So much time and toil they gave,
In hopes of a time more lively and less grey.

To take it all away, to crush their hope,
To send them back to the endless void.

Aren't we all just chemical romances?
Bodies of reactions devoid of purpose.

So what if a murder is alright?
To kill what should have died on its own?

Or is it not for us to choose?
The blade of fate not for ours to wield.

Their ashes not for us to spread,
To the lifeless void of this endless sea!

Fake Lines

To force myself upon a poem,
To drag it out without my consent.

To spill a few words of whimsical tone,
A grammatical jumble to add to its flow.

Diverse words provide for pretentious flavour,
Vague emotions provide for the spark of a reader's
heart.

How dishonest, filthy and perverse?
To seek admiration most undeserved!

A tough word to boggle the mind of the beholder,
A flimsy metaphor to add to its facade of a splendour.

Of uneven form, a false lie to its free form.
Of dishonest lines, so blank, rigid, and forced.

A disgrace to poetry, a stain on its soul,
An addition unworthy of bare mediocrity.

A spit in the face of peers, if any,
A bare minimum remains out of bare humility.

A liar, a thief, a fake and an impostor,
There is no redemption from this pompous display of
a poet.

Of Statues in the Nude

To gaze upon the statues of nude bodies,
To lay eyes upon their elegance and revered beauty.

Obscene to most, vulgar to a few,
Yet to an artist, a beauty transcending heavenly
allure.

The curves and the edges, so smooth and so lively,
The muscles of the form, radiating all glamour.

A painstaking masterpiece, the human form.
In all its glory, baring it all.

There is no shame presented, no vulgarity intended.
For beauty is always in the eyes of the beholder.

The human form, in its naked brilliance,
A show of strength, of Godly might.

In its bare essence, language becomes of power.
In its freedom, never forgotten for all eternity.

Carved in stone, of every feature,
An artist's masterpiece, for the world to see.

The Love Letter

Entwined in a fiery bond are two hearts, or maybe
more,
Of minds that yearn to be closer to one another,
forever more.

Of the hearts in love, all passion is drawn,
All their love flowed into the eternal abyss.

To lay their eyes on one another,
To hear what the other one speaks.

To feel the warmth and joy, of each other's heat.
To be in slumber in the arms of the other.

To feel the heart thicken at the sound of their voice.
To feel your insides spiral in a shivering rush.

Does a letter hold the essence of their love?
An expression of their deepest regard for the other?

Do the words need be beautiful?
Of most verbose with the complexity of love itself.

Does the tone need be melodious?
Sung from the voices of most grace?

With a pen of envious calligraphy?
With meanings of impossible proportions?

Or could the words be small and their meanings so
simple?
Yet it's the one who writes it what matters most.

Is it the simple act of having said it,
The most beautiful form of love?

Could the love letter possess just a word,
And yet fill the lovers to their hearts' content?

Does one have to love to know this feeling?
To know of romance to comprehend its beauty.

No, it cannot be defined with a simple equation,
For love is most complex, and yet so simple.

Loneliness

Keep me on an empty island.
No one to talk to, no one to meet.

Makes no difference to a man,
Who prefers to be lonely.

An auteur of his own life,
With no other people to indulge with.

A man of his own thoughts,
The most dangerous state to exist.

He's discouraged by none,
He's encouraged by all.

His ideas often violent, or maybe of peace,
Wisdom of a sage or the cunning of a narcissist.

His thoughts are his friends, his sole solace.
It either imprisons him or sets him free.

What is loneliness, a phase or a condition?
To not have a friend, to talk to at your side.

Does one spin off into madness?
Into thoughts that end in misery and regret.

To end one's life for being in solitary,
And yet, to have none to bid farewell to.

Such is the fate for the lonely man,
For he lives in solace and dies in solitude.

Envy

How would it feel,
To be in the skin of a woman?

To be feminine,
To be more cute than handsome?

How would it feel to be more gentle?
To be of pure heart and innocent eyes?

How would it feel, to wear dresses and skirts?
To have no thoughts about the ones around.

How would it feel, to wear your hair out?
To have skin so smooth, silky and comforting?

How does it feel, to be a woman trapped in a man?
To have your body never be truly yours?

To have to be tough, when you need to be gentle.
To have to be stoic, when you need to be vulnerable.

How does it feel, to have to prove,
You're more manly, than the one next to you?

Why do you have to be a man to be brave?
Why do you have to be so rough to win?

Throw away your blades, and unclench your fists.
Shed your armour and let your bare body replace it.

They dare deny you what is rightfully yours?
To be a woman in spite of a man's body.

To be a woman when the others say,
"You will never be…"

An act so brave,
A man could never be.

Flaunt your form to the entire world,
Let them speak ill, to be in disgust.

As brave as you are,
They could never be.

Be the woman you are,
And leave them to their envy.

No Deeds Here Lie

I must walk the path,
with gaze towards a starless sky.

So dark the journey with wrath,
Yet no redemption lay bare.

Fare myself to the earth,
Where ghosts of past lie.

No songs were sung to my worth,
No hymns that cast my dye.

What is life to man but a path to death,
Yet no deeds for man here lie.

The Cold Blade

The razor gleams in the dim-lit room,
The faint shine feels so cold to the sight.

A million threads yarned in a loom,
And only doom it could conjure in my plight.

A hundred cries heard from the door,
A million tears in vain for my demise.

The steel is cold against my skin,
A cold lover yearning for my warmth.

A slice of nerve; a kiss of death,
Seducing me in the brim of the dying light.

The light has passed in its empty heave,
The faint cry, no longer heard.

The air so dark fills into me,
The blade slits my skin with its nimble lust.

The gushing warmth is freeing,
An embrace of warmth, of impending release.

Yet my eyes bleed in cold,
An ode to the freezing world.

Take me there, where all thoughts run
unshackled,
A place of tranquil, of everlasting emptiness.

Take my thoughts, and my warmth,
Give me peace, and bring me closer to the dark.

The Grind

The wheels have never stopped turning,
A useless loop moving along the dry earth.

My head grows dizzy, my eyes tear up blurry,
A voice screams out to me, "Stop."

Was stopping ever the problem? A suspended
disbelief!
It has always been a way out.

My heart beats slower, my joints give away,
It's tiring to keep up with the pace.

I cannot keep on, this parched earth so barren.
The salt has dried me up in full.

The rain offers a warning, a temporary relief.
It warns of the impending heat in approach.

Joy has left me, crumbling in my steps.
Lust never craves for me, a sigh of regret.

My eyes are blurry no more, they don't hurt.
Blindness has folded me in its drapes of secrets.

The icy touch shivers my core, a cold sweat in
its trace.
I'm tired of running away, away from the weight
of it all.

Everything feels so permanent,
Yet in the end, it's all so temporary.

It's time for me to go, to leave it all behind.
Without saying "Goodbye."

Vast Horizons

In the tall peak I stood,
Hands with blood dripping down.

Nothing ever really goes away,
They all come flowing down.

I took my final stand,
Lamenting over the paths I crossed.

Most being joyful,
Yet none to be content.

Are all the flowers in the valley,
Blooming with the salt of my sorrows?

Do their beauty draw my eyes
From the disfigured ground beneath?

Or did I do it all for naught?
A whole life of drag, tensed strings pulling me
back.

Is this Nirvana? My final redemption.
Or is this Hell? My ultimate downfall.

Is it all really over? My endless toil.
Am I finally free of it all?

The vast horizons stretched before my eyes to
behold.
My eyes have no salt to soothe the pain of my
tears.

The final breath, so eager, yet calm,
Washes over me with a dreadful peace.

Oh, to have lived a life with happiness and
regrets,
Where one overshadowed the other overall.

To fall for a Dame

Of beauties, I gazed upon thee,
And pondered upon my gaze.

Fairness and strength I saw in thee,
Of which none to be seen in me.

Oh, the envy of strength, of Herculean might,
I stare at thee with a hopeless sigh.

To avert my gaze would be a crime,
For such beauty is truly a sign of the Gods.

To look upon thy heart, and to feel love,
Blinded not by lust, but by love herself.

For years, I will yearn for this feeling to come.
Yet always will I be stopped by the guilt of my
flesh.

To love thee not for thy glory, but for thee in thy
true self.
To enjoy not the pleasures of thy body, but the
presence of thy mind.

Not to is a shame, one I will carry in thy name.
My heart has fallen for thee, and has fallen shut
for all but thee.

Oh Goddess Palaestra, of unmatched strength
and vigour,
I fall at your feet, to behold your might and
beauty.

What lies beyond the Deep?

I grip the pipe fence ever so tightly,
And lean to see what lies before me.

The dark blue ocean lays stretched,
As far as the eye could see.

The pull of the ship gives my steps a twitch,
My grip turns tighter as my breathing starts to
deepen.

Staring at the dark sea, with the stars above me,
I feel as if I'm staring at a reflection of the sky.

Could it be that my voyage is through the deep
space,
With an endless abyss of starry skies above and
below.

The vastness brings me shivers,
And along with it, its horrors.

I wonder if something lies beyond,
Beyond what the eye could see.

Something so vast and mighty,
It would swallow us all, never to be seen any
more.

We have charted the skies, we have wandered
the earth,
And yet, of the Sea, spoils still remain.

What lost treasures, what sunken ships,
What forgotten myths, what mineral riches.

Or could it hold horrors beyond what we have
seen,
Of gigantic creatures bigger than a whale,

Rising to swallow us up whole,
And never to be seen of again.

What truly lies beyond the Deep,
We may never truly know for years to come.

The Eyes

The eyes, to me, never cease to amaze.
Their structure and form, so complex and alluring.

So fragile, yet so drawing.
Its beauty, truly a "sight" to behold.

They form in such colours -
Black, blue, green and hazel.

With a tinge of red peeking about,
The eye truly is a feat so magnificent.

Eyes sad with tears are so hauntingly beautiful,
For only in the darkest of times, does burn with
vigour the light.

The eyes may mirror the intentions of the mind,
For the ones that hypnotise you, might hold sinister
thoughts.

To stare into your eyes is a Herculean task,
As it is to look into your soul, without the faintest
disregard.

The patterns of your iris pulls me to a trance
To lay a night in those flaming embers.

What are we?

What are we, if not human?
Every one of us, more equal than different.

How am I different, with the colour of my skin?
The melanin never held the reins of my fate.

How am I different, with the money in my
name?
A false concept, taken away as quickly as it is
given.

How am I different, to the place where I was
born?
If not one place, then the other, truly all the
same.

How am I different, to the god that I pray?
If a god divides me from you, then both our gods
are truly false.

How am I different, for the tongue in which I
speak?
For all it's ever worth, is a matter of
comprehension.

How am I different, for the one I choose to love?
For my love is true, and it can never be corroded
with hate.

How am I different, for how I feel inside?
For if I was born in a different body, doesn't
make me any different from you.

If these are what divides me from you,
Then are you even human to divide me at all?

To deny me the pleasure of being human,
What do you gain from your irrational need for
division?

A false creed, a false religion, a false supremacy,
And bloodshed to lay ground for your unholy
crusade.

Fall to the earth and see for yourself,
From ashes, we arose and to ashes back, we fall
again.

Our ashes are same, no matter the one,
Your doctrines too, lost to time.

All that blood has stained the earth,
And no longer human, you have become.

Zero to Midnight

An apocalypse is nigh, with no escape in sight.
We watch as the sky is filled with shooting stars so
bright.

An entire planet at each others' throats,
Racing to see who could collapse under itself first.

A bomb that kills a million people,
Why do we need it? Nobody cared to answer!

A system draining its mass for a few,
Why did we need it? Nobody cared to notice!

A girl who stood up to demand a future,
Laughed at and told to go back to her place.

A man so false and cruelly parasitic,Hailed as a
saviour and a beacon of hope.

People of science, giving their lives to warn us,
Did we ever look up and heed what they said?

To have had so much, we could have bettered
ourselves,
Yet wasted in the name of comfort and greed!

There is no saviour at the end, no failsafe button.
It's every man for himself to the death.

How did we get here? Why did we lose?
Our own species dug our own graves.

If only we had widened our gaze, with our eyes to the
sky,
We could have ventured further, our fate in the stars.

Yet we stand here now, bombing each other,
All at the grand whims of cowards in power!

We mistook greed for ambition, force for power,
Ignorance for common sense, hate for righteousness.

Look where we stand, look how we've fallen,
How shameful it is to call ourselves the apex
primates.

The Doomsday Clocked has stroked midnight
And here we lay to rest, an entire legacy, in ashes of
plight.

An Idea for a Poem

To what shall I owe the pleasure today,
For a poem, what ideas do I spare today?

To seek a good thought, an idea, so timeless and
original.
To wander far into the depths, failing to see what
hides in plain sight.

Is it the idea that makes the poem, or is it vice
versa?
Is it the lines that make up the words, or is it
vice versa?

What words do I use to tell you what I mean?
To make you feel exactly as I do?

What lines do I craft to frame its rhythm?
To make you dance to the tunes of my heart?

What thoughts do I instil to frame its logic?
To make you think exactly like I did?

What makes a poem so different,
from a thought with rhythm recited?

Is it the form or the essence of the poem itself?
Is it the rhythm or the flow of the words inside?

A poem can be mediocre or great,
No matter the words, the lines or the rhythm.

A poem has a soul, and the soul reigns supreme.
To understand it is to be one with the poem.

If passion and art were in vain, yet reverence so
undeservingly great,
The poem has gained a crooked soul, deceiving,
even in mediocrity.

To write a few lines, a simple task.
To make it a poem, a Herculean one.

There are more forces at play than words or
meanings,
All in turn, adorned by its soul supreme.

An idea for a poem can be simple or great,
It's the soul that marks its entire fate.

www.ingramcontent.com/pod-product-compliance
Lightning Source LLC
La Vergne TN
LVHW010925200726
843509LV00013B/2070